Skills for OU Study

Studying with Dyslexia

The Open University Walton Hall, Milton Keynes MK7 6AA

The Open University is incorporated by Royal Charter (RC 000391), an exempt charity in England & Wales and a charity registered in Scotland (SC 038302).

Edited, designed and typeset by The Open University.

Printed in the United Kingdom by Thanet Press.

ISBN 978-0-7492-2918-4

1.1

Skills for OU Study

Studying with Dyslexia

Dyslexia can reveal itself in many different ways as you study. In this booklet you will find strategies for learning and tips for making your study pathway smoother. This booklet accompanies the *Skills for OU Study* website http://www.open.ac.uk/skillsforstudy, which contains advice, quizzes and exercises to help you.

Contents

1	Introduction	7
2	What is dyslexia?	8
3	Learning at the OU	12
4	Organisation and time management	17
5	Reading	22
6	Taking notes	25
7	Assignment writing	29
8	Revision and exams	33
9	In conclusion	40
Reference		40

1 Introduction

This booklet is for Open University (OU) students who may or may not have a formal diagnosis of dyslexia. It describes some of the challenges of studying with dyslexia and aims to help you to develop effective skills for studying with the OU.

Use the sections you need and write on the book or add ideas wherever you like. It's yours to use in the best way for you.

Further information

You will find additional resources on the StudentHome site www.open.ac.uk/students, such as links to *Skills for OU Study*, *Careers Advisory Service* and a guide to *Assessment*. You will also find details of *Services for Disabled Students*.

If you need to talk to somebody about your study and/or additional needs, you will find contact details at the back of your Welcome Booklet.

2 What is dyslexia?

Dyslexia is a specific learning difference that can impact on the way individuals learn, and which is experienced by each individual differently.

The definition of dyslexia has changed over the years and no single definition is universally accepted. In early childhood, dyslexia may be suspected 'when accurate and fluent reading and/or spelling develops very incompletely or with great difficulty' (British Psychological Society, 1999, p. 64). You may be able to identify with this definition from your own experience as a child. In adults, the OU recognises dyslexia as characterised by an unusual balance of skills, each individual having their own profile of strengths and weakness.

Research into the causes of dyslexia continues and various theories exist. However, there is general agreement that the dyslexic brain processes some information in a different way from other brains, affecting language, short-term memory and retrieval of information. The difference gives clear advantages in some cognitive and creative areas, though it can also create difficulties. The difficulties arise because dyslexic people operate in a world in which communication has developed to suit the non-dyslexic majority. Now that we know this, it is more acceptable to 'identify' rather than to 'diagnose' dyslexia.

2.1 What are the effects of dyslexia?

Each individual experiences the impact of dyslexia differently. Some people will have had a positive experience and learned to recognise their strengths; some will have had a more negative experience. Some people will have had the opportunity to develop compensatory strategies, others won't.

The main areas where the impact can be felt are in:

- reading, which is likely to be slow
- concentration, which tends to fluctuate
- spelling and grammar, which can be unorthodox
- physical coordination and handwriting, which can be inconsistent and untidy
- remembering information, which can be better some days than others

- organising and planning, which can make the management of learning materials more demanding than expected
- working within time limits, which can be stressful in exams
- thinking and working in sequences, which can make planning challenging
- visual difficulties, such as blurring and distortion of print
- visual processing difficulties, which can make reading uncomfortable
- auditory processing difficulties, which can make listening to oral instructions tiring and confusing.

About one person in ten of the general population has trouble with spelling and memory, but about one in 25 experiences difficulties that have a moderate to serious effect on their whole lives. These people are less likely to achieve their full potential unless they develop compensating strategies and have appropriate support and encouragement.

2.2 What you can do

By now you may have started to think about your own skills and your previous experiences. Table 1 (overleaf) will help you to consider your current strengths and weaknesses.

2.3 Applying for the Disabled Student's Allowance

The Disabled Student's Allowance (DSA) is a government-funded grant awarded to people with disabilities that impact on their learning.

OU students in England, Wales, Northern Ireland and Scotland, who have a full assessment (see below) clearly identifying dyslexia, may be eligible for a DSA. Details are sent to students who have told the OU that they are dyslexic.

The DSA can be used to pay for equipment and facilities related to your dyslexia, but not for the cost of identifying it.

Please contact your regional or national centre to discuss how to obtain a full assessment or to let us know that you are dyslexic.

Table 1 Think about your study skills

Study area	What other students have said	Our tips
Reading	"It seems to take me much longer than anyone else – I have to reread everything several times." "I simply can't remember what a word looks like."	Review the section on reading in this booklet Consider exploring audio materials Use text-to-speech software
Written work	"I never seem to be able to put down what I am thinking." "I know what I want to say but I can't find the right words."	Review your planning strategies and try out new styles. For example, you may like to use mind maps or PowerPoint for planning assignments
Presentation of written work, grammar	"Proofreading is a nightmare – I spend hours looking words up, again and again. I still miss things and I can't always work out what I was trying to write."	Build up a checklist to use at the stage of editing after the first draft
Handwriting and notes	"My handwriting is horrible and I have always struggled with exams." "I write really slowly."	Try out different pens Review note-taking strategies Discuss access arrangements for exams with your regional or national centre.
Spelling and vocabulary	"Sometimes I spell a word correctly and in the very next sentence, misspell it. But both spellings look the same to me." "I feel so embarrassed about my spelling – and worry that tutors will think I am lazy as they did at school."	Build up a vocabulary list Learn to use Auto Correct in your word processing software Contact your tutor to discuss any concerns you might have about your spelling
Note taking	"I can't read my own notes most of the time." "I start taking notes, but trying to spell words correctly is so tiring, I never get very far."	Try using mind maps, or recording audio notes
Organisation	"Finding different forms, assignment booklets, timetables for tutorials etc. is chaotic. Information seems to be stored in several different places and if I put it down in the wrong place that's it."	Follow the simple guidelines in this booklet to start getting organised
Oral skills	"I really worry about making contributions in tutorials."	Go to Skills for OU Study to pick up tips about discussion and presentation skills

2.4 The full assessment for dyslexia

A full assessment can be carried out by an educational psychologist or a suitably qualified professional, such as a teacher who has the Diploma in Specific Learning Difficulties. During the assessment you have an opportunity to discuss your learning history and do a range of tests selected to build up a picture of your learning strengths and weaknesses. The whole process can take up to three hours. A report is then prepared for you that outlines the results of the tests and explains your learning profile.

When might a full assessment be necessary or of value?

A 'full assessment' is essential if you wish to apply for a Disabled Student's Allowance or for access arrangements for exams, such as extra time or use of a word processor.

A full assessment can help you to understand how you learn best, make sense of your past learning experience, and help you plan for successful study (see Figure 1).

However, whether or not to take the assessment is an individual decision. Some people with dyslexia choose not to be formally assessed and prefer to take their own approach and explore learning in their own way.

If you would like to discuss your choice then a good first step is to talk to a member of your regional or national Disability and Additional Requirements (DAR) Team.

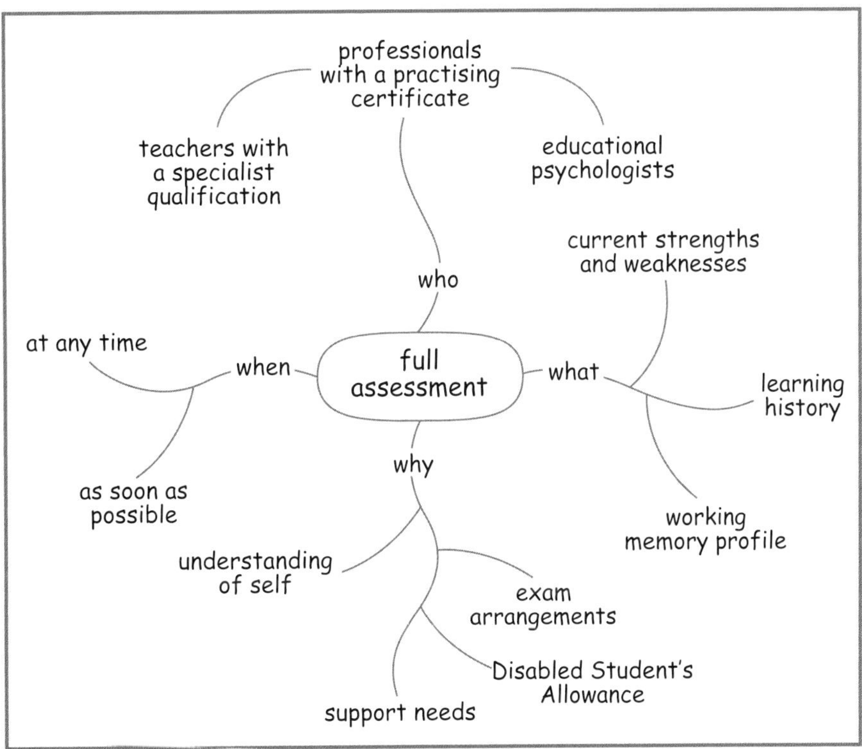

Figure 1 The elements of a full assessment

3 Learning at the OU

OU students are sent course materials to study, which could be printed and arrive through the post or be available online. Each course also uses other media, such as audio or video recordings. Courses may include software to use on your computer or online resources such as a course forum where you can discuss your study and work with other students. Because the different materials are combined with support from a tutor or student adviser and the student services staff, the OU approach is called 'supported open learning'.

During your course you learn through reading course material, working on course activities, writing assignments and perhaps working with other students (see Figure 2).

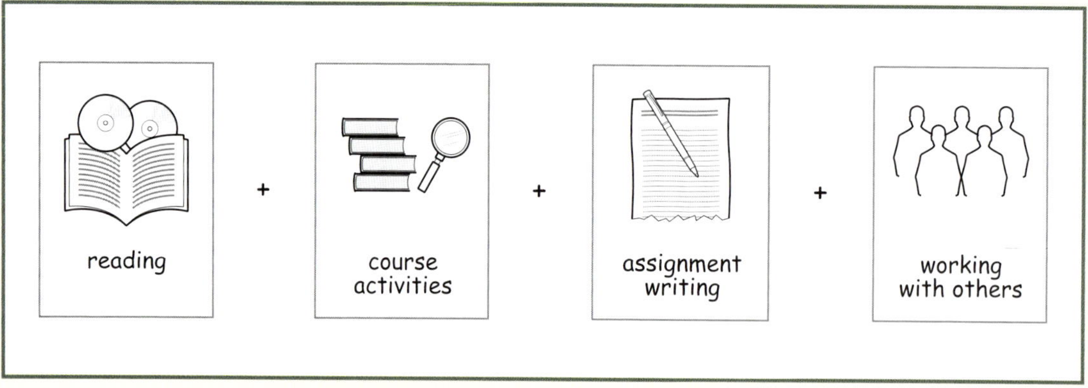

Figure 2 These are the things you will be doing during your course

The assignments you complete throughout the course help to keep you on schedule, and by submitting them to your tutor you receive regular feedback on your progress. Most assignments are graded and count towards your final continuous assessment score, but they also help you to learn.

OU tutorials can be face-to-face or conducted online. Students find that tutorials are a great opportunity to raise their own questions and difficulties, as well as meet other people studying the course.

3.1 The challenges you might face

You will need to be organised to make sure that you are working on the right course material and that you send in your assignments on time.You'll have quite a lot of reading to do, and will need to make notes so that you can learn from the course material. You will also have assignments to plan and prepare.

There are lots of different contexts for your learning, and some will be more difficult for you than others. Table 2 shows different situations and possible challenges you may experience.

Table 2 Learning contexts and challenges

Context	Challenges
Face-to-face tutorial	Writing notes, sharing ideas
Online tutorial or online forum	Writing your responses to messages
Course desktop	Finding the resources you need
Residential or day school	Working with different people, sharing ideas
Tutor marked assignment (TMA)	Preparing written work
Computer marked assignment (CMA)	Choosing from multiple answers
Examination	Working under timed conditions
Oral exam	Remembering what you need to say
End of course assessment (ECA)	Presenting written work

3.2 What you can do

Plan ahead

Use your course calendar and study guide. They give a vital overview of the work you will do and when the assignments are due. Keep to the schedule and you will be on track.

Develop your computer skills

You may find that using a word processor helps you to produce your printed work, because it can minimise some of the problems associated with spelling and handwriting. It can also make structuring and planning assignments more manageable.

If you plan to take an online course you should have some basic skills first, so that the technology doesn't interfere with your subject learning. You should be able to:

- manage files
- navigate the internet
- use email and attachments.

Even if you are studying a course that uses printed materials, you should expect to work on a computer for your assignments and to use online resources from the OU. See more on page 19 about working with your computer.

Learning preferences

No one person learns in exactly the same way as another. We do, however, fall into overlapping groups of learning styles, and it's very useful to be aware of your own group. It's particularly important if you're dyslexic. To understand how you learn and to know something about your preferred learning style is to recognise an area of strength.

We learn through our senses: by seeing, hearing, doing, touching, smelling. The last three are usually grouped together as 'kinaesthetic' or 'tactile' learning. A multisensory learner will use the senses equally, or use them all across the various kinds of learning. Most of us use one or two of the senses more effectively than the others.

Because the dyslexic brain tends to have a more developed right side, the side that deals with patterns and spatial awareness, you may have a tendency to be a holistic rather than a linear thinker – you work better from an overall picture than from a step-by-step (linear) process. You may be intuitive rather than deductive, perhaps reaching conclusions without knowing how or why. You may remember things in patterns instead of sequences. In fact you probably have difficulty remembering sequences such as the alphabet or telephone numbers. This may lead you to remember things by making connections that aren't apparent to other people. Your spatial awareness – the ability to know how things might look from any direction – may be particularly good.

Take some time to reflect on your learning strengths and preferences. Use the information on the *Skills for OU Study* website at www.open.ac.uk/skillsforstudy to help you consider your strengths and how effectively you use them.

3.3 How the OU can help

The OU has staff in all regional and national centres who can advise on matters relating to your study at the OU. Each centre has a Disability and Additional Requirements Team, whose staff can offer specific advice in relation to your individual need. In some instances they are able to arrange for additional sessions in which you can discuss your studying in more depth.

As a registered student you have access to online study support through StudentHome. This site is your gateway to a range of resources that support your study, and it includes information on your personal study record, the schedule of activities in your course, and links to study skills information.

At the level of course materials, your course guide gives you an overview of the course, its ideas and themes. It also tells you about the learning materials you will use. It usually contains advice and guidance on how to approach each section of material.

If alternative course materials would suit you better, check with your Disability and Additional Requirements Team to see whether they are available for your course, or check on the Services for Disabled Students website, which you can access through StudentHome.

How your tutor can help

Your tutor may not know a great deal about dyslexia. However, they will have a general awareness. If you can explain what some of the difficulties might be, you will be able to work out some strategies that will help you in your studies.

Make a short list of the things that you find hardest. Start by putting a tick against any of the remarks on the list below that you think might be issues for you, and discuss these with your tutor.

- I take ages reading.
- I don't know what to say in the online discussion.
- The reading is taking me so long I am worried I will get behind.
- I find it difficult to make notes.
- I can't read my notes back afterwards – they don't seem to make sense.
- I find it hard to follow the discussion and to join in.
- I really hate to read something aloud.
- I am scared I will spell it all badly if I write something on an online forum.
- I am not really sure how to do lots of things on the computer.
- I know what to say but I can't write it down.
- Organisation is a nightmare – I don't know how to file everything.
- I read something and still don't get the hang of it after half an hour.

There are more ideas that will help you with your learning on the *Skills for OU Study* website at www.open.ac.uk/skillsforstudy

Although your tutor cannot help you to write your assignments, he or she can organise an extra session to go over what you have written in a previous assignment and explain what is working and what isn't. It can be helpful to spend time discussing the feedback they have written on your assignment. An extra session can also be used to go over parts of the course you are finding difficult. Your tutor may be able to help you identify the absolutely essential reading and what might be left until later.

Top tip

Keep in touch with your tutor. This is especially important if you feel you are starting to fall behind. A quick telephone call or an email can make all the difference.

4 Organisation and time management

OU students have to keep track of a lot of material. Some of it is course material, either printed or online. You also get information to help you work through the course, such as a study calendar or planner, a course guide and an assignment guide. There is also information about your study with the OU, such as payments made and records of the courses you have studied and chosen.

> ‘I like to be organised. I know it takes me a long time to do all the reading and I have to think about this at the beginning of the course. Not just the time for reading, but also how and when I am going to make and store my notes. Once I'm organised I feel much more in control. I plan my time carefully and can juggle work, studying and children. Well, most of the time!’

4.1 The challenges you might face

Many students find it difficult to keep track of the various kinds of material. Course material sometimes gets mixed in with important reminders for assignments, or perhaps with course choice papers that should be sent to the OU.

If you normally find it difficult to manage your time then you may find that this is particularly challenging at the OU, where you don't have much opportunity for personal reminders through face-to-face contact with your tutor or other students.

Juggling study time and other commitments such as work, family and regular leisure activities can be demanding. You do need a lot of self discipline in order to be successful.

4.2 What you can do

Good study habits make a big difference to your learning. Good organisation can help reduce the amount you have to remember. Students with dyslexia often find that it helps to be even more organised than other students, but you may first need to develop the strategies required (see Figure 3).

It is well worth spending some time thinking through the skills you use now, in different areas of your life. You may be surprised at how many strategies you do have already. Whether you are organising something to a deadline, such as a holiday, or dealing with everyday paperwork at work or at home, you already use some planning and organisational strategies. Try to list some of these strategies and consider which could be useful for OU study. Perhaps you already chunk your shopping list under sub-headings, which is a useful strategy for planning an assignment. Maybe you record dates and events on a calendar in your mobile phone, which you can continue to do for managing study deadlines.

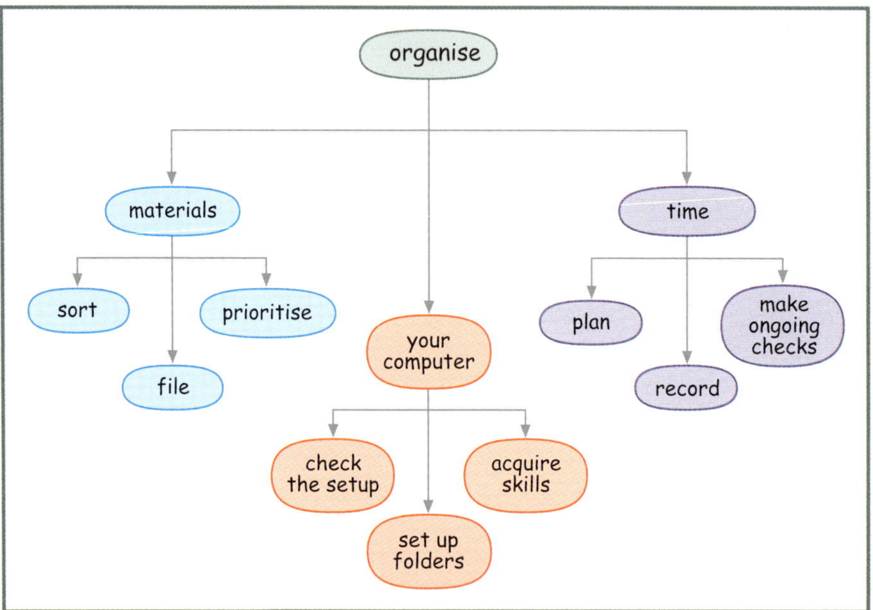

Figure 3 You will need to organise your course materials, your computer files and your time during your studies

Organise your materials

Deal with printed materials as soon as they arrive. Check the contents list to see that everything is there then look through to see what should be kept. If you have letters or emails that need a reply, try to respond to them straight away so that a backlog doesn't build up and you don't miss deadlines.

File things in the correct place straight away. Your materials will come in all shapes and sizes, and there'll be a lot. One way to make them more manageable is by colour coding. You could put a green label or small sticker on everything to do with course materials, for example, and a red one on everything to do with administration, or have different colours to split the course materials into different topics. If folders, books, notes, file cards, audio materials are all marked in this way, you can easily find the materials you need for the task in hand.

> ‘Plastic storage boxes are my thing. I fill my dining room with different coloured boxes and use a different one for each module.’

Your information – everything you need to learn and remember – is much more manageable if you pick out the most important things and make them easy to find.

Set up your computer

Make sure your word processor is set up to suit your needs. Here are some options.

- Place your screen where it is free of reflections, and adjust its brightness and contrast.
- Adjust the colour of the text and the background.
- Select the font style and size.
- Use Zoom to make the ‘page’ on your screen whatever size you find easiest to work with.
- Left-justify your text (as in this book). Many dyslexic people find that this helps to overcome visual distortion.
- Use the keyboard or the mouse, whichever you prefer.
- Set up Auto Correct to deal with errors you’re particularly likely to make, and to complete words and phrases you type in frequently.
- AutoText (in Microsoft Word) enables you to store text (such as your address or student details), and even images, for insertion into any document.
- Add more control buttons on the toolbar, to save hunting through the menus.
- Create a template if you’re going to produce several documents of a similar kind.

Organise your computer files

Sorting out your electronic filing system before you start your studies can really help. Think through what folders you may need. It helps to use multiple folders to organise work, with sub folders for different areas, and you can add more later if you need them (see Figure 4).

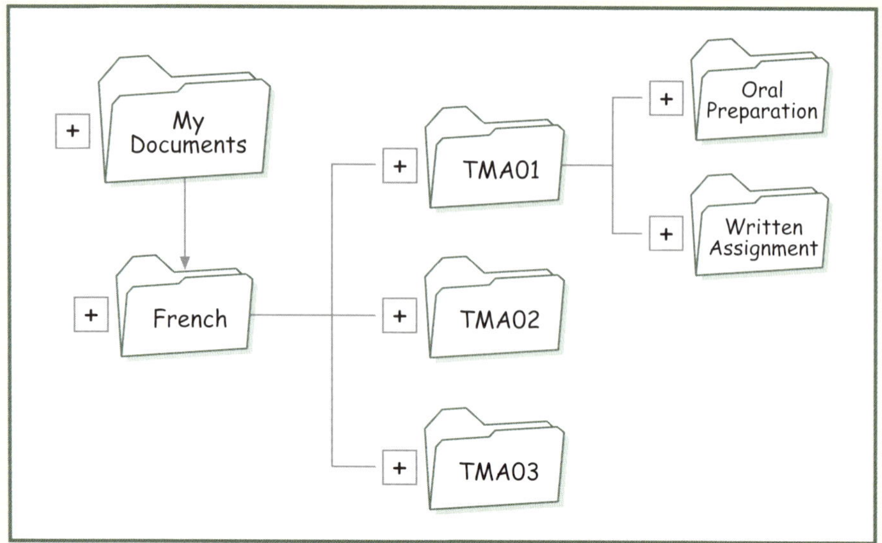

Figure 4 Organising your electronic documents into a clear folder structure on your computer will help you find things quickly later on during your studies

You can find out more about making folders and using your word processor on the *Skills for OU Study* website at www.open.ac.uk/skillsforstudy.

If you prefer verbal records to text, you may like to consider using speech recognition software and/or a digital voice recorder. These can be useful for assignment writing and note taking at tutorials. A word of warning, though – software takes some time to learn to use effectively and you may need a lot of training. It is not for everyone, but if you think this might be useful you can find up-to-date information on the web.

Top tip

Always keep an exact copy of your submitted TMA.

Organise your time

Finding and organising time for study is a challenge for every student, but can be an even bigger one if you are dyslexic. You might be wise to allow twice the recommended time for each new study task, at least during your first course. Allowing extra time will relieve the pressure and give you scope for developing new strategies.

Having a clear idea of when you are most likely to find time to work does help.

All courses have a calendar or planner, sometimes on paper but always on the course website. Make sure you know where it is so that you keep the deadlines in mind. You might keep a copy on a wall in your study area or in the kitchen.

Add extra detail to your calendar. Look at the deadline for your first assignment and plan backwards from this, working out a realistic time for completing each stage (see page 30).

You could discuss the deadlines with your tutor or study adviser at the beginning of your course so you can both identify effective strategies.

Organise a working space

You don't have to be super-tidy to study effectively. You could be surrounded by apparent chaos, so long as it doesn't interfere with what you want to achieve. Many people feel more comfortable with chaos than with clinical tidiness.

Choose and organise a working space to suit your preferences. Here are a few ideas to think about or to adapt.

Your study area ideally should be a place where:

- you can leave things and they won't be moved
- there's as little distraction as possible (choose, for example, a quiet room)
- the temperature is comfortable
- there's space for a worktop, filing, shelves and a notice board
- you can put up a large wall calendar, with colour-coded stickers for assignment dates, tutorials, exams and so on.

In reality you may have to manage with less than this, but once you have established your study place, make a habit of using it regularly.

There are more ideas about organisation and time management on the *Skills for OU Study* website at www.open.ac.uk/skillsforstudy

5 Reading

Studying as a distance learner with the OU means more reading, on paper or on computer screen, than might be necessary at other institutions, where there are greater opportunities to learn from tutors and lecturers in person. OU reading material is carefully selected, so you'll spend less time searching for the relevant articles and information. The work is also more structured, with clear instructions for study tasks and suggestions for allotting time to them, and as a dyslexic student you'll probably find that helpful too.

5.1 The challenges you might face

Many students with dyslexia can read reasonably well and have developed their own compensating strategies, even if they struggled with reading as children. However, sometimes reading continues to be a challenging and time-consuming activity. The challenges vary according to an individual's experience and processing profile.

5.2 What you can do

Go for essential reading first and start with material that isn't too challenging. Accept that it may not be necessary to read everything provided. If you are at all unsure ask your tutor for advice on essential and non-essential reading.

> ‘I find that I have to plan in extra time for reading. The first time I read a passage I concentrate on the decoding, on checking whether I can read all the words. It is only on the second or third reading that I start to unpick the meaning.’

Allow additional time for reading. Being more realistic about the time your reading takes will help your study planning.

Make use of any specialist glossaries included in your course materials. Print off a copy of each glossary and keep them to hand. Familiarity with the key vocabulary really helps when you are reading and thinking about your course.

Change the appearance of electronic text to make it more comfortable to read. On the *Skills for OU Study* website at www.open.ac.uk/skillsforstudy you can find out how to change:

- the colour of the letters
- the colour of the background
- the font style
- the size of the letters
- line spacing – try 1.5.

If you are reading printed material you can also change the look of the document to make it more comfortable to read. Changing the contrast between print and print background can make a huge difference. Here are some ideas.

- Try out coloured overlays, available from some high street stationers.
- Try printing out materials on different coloured paper.
- Make copies of double sided materials so that there is less page turning involved.
- Make hard copies of electronic materials so that you can add your own notes.

If reading continues to be uncomfortable then consider visiting an optometrist, who can assess and prescribe for specific needs such as scotopic sensitivity. Scotopic sensitivity can be the cause of visual discomfort and print instability. A white page may glare, causing eye strain or headaches. Words may appear to move, to jumble or to blur. Shadows may seem to fall across the page. All this interferes with reading, and is likely to reduce your attention and concentration.

> ‘I find that the print can appear to blur, lines appear to move. I end up having to concentrate really hard.’

Listening to the text can also be useful. The spoken text can help you with:

- comprehension and concentration
- pronunciation of new and unfamiliar words
- skim-reading
- proof-reading your own work.

Some students find that reading aloud aids concentration and understanding. Other students use software that enables you to listen to all electronic materials including your own writing, course material and electronically researched material.

Reading online

Online forums are an increasingly valuable part of our learning experience. However, it can be time consuming to keep track of all the activity on a forum. Remember that you don't need to read every message that is posted.

Reading for meaning

What works for you? Students sometimes say that they read and read, but don't seem to be able to take anything in. If you have had a similar experience, then review your strategies and consider some of the suggestions on the *Skills for OU Study* website at www.open.ac.uk/skillsforstudy

6 Taking notes

6.1 The challenges you might face

Good note taking is a key to successful studying. Taking notes usually means doing several tasks at the same time – listening or reading, understanding, summarising, writing. These activities place a lot of demand on the working memory if you're dyslexic. You may be more confident in one area than in others.

6.2 What you can do

Remember, the purpose of note taking is to enable you to recall the key vocabulary and concepts. Over 90 per cent of written notes taken by students are superfluous. This is good news for students with dyslexia – notes do not require a lot of writing, but they do demand skill. Be prepared to be creative and have fun.

> *'One of the hard things is choosing which are the important bits of what I'm reading. With course materials I read a few paragraphs or a page, then summarise that in a short sentence in the margin. That way I can look through the pages at my short notes, rather than having to read all the text again.'*

Sometimes we take notes so that we'll have a written record of something we've read. But there are other kinds of notes too. You might write out a shopping list, or instructions for finding your way somewhere. You may throw notes away when they've served their purpose. You might write notes that help you to make links in your head between ideas. Making notes helps you to concentrate, and forces you to prioritise the important points. Notes of that kind are not intended as a record, but are a means of clarifying your thoughts.

Taking notes can help you in several ways.

- Concentrating – the process of thinking and writing can help you to focus your attention and so to learn more effectively.
- Remembering – writing something down can help you to remember it. You can also refer back to it to check your memory.
- Understanding – making rough notes or a diagram can help you to 'unpack' complex parts of your reading material.

- Keeping a record – of talks, tutorials, broadcasts, things you need to do.
- Summarising – the key points of procedures, course units and so on. Try choosing any passage from a text and writing down five points made in it. Then try linking them in continuous prose, for writing practice. This may be something that a tutor can help you with in an additional session.
- Reordering or organising materials in a way that suits your learning style and picks out the things you need to learn.
- Highlighting key points or ideas so that you can refer to them later.
- Planning – notes are a good way to start off your ideas for an assignment.
- Developing your reading vocabulary – listing new terminology on paper or electronically (try your mobile phone) can help you develop your reading and writing skills.

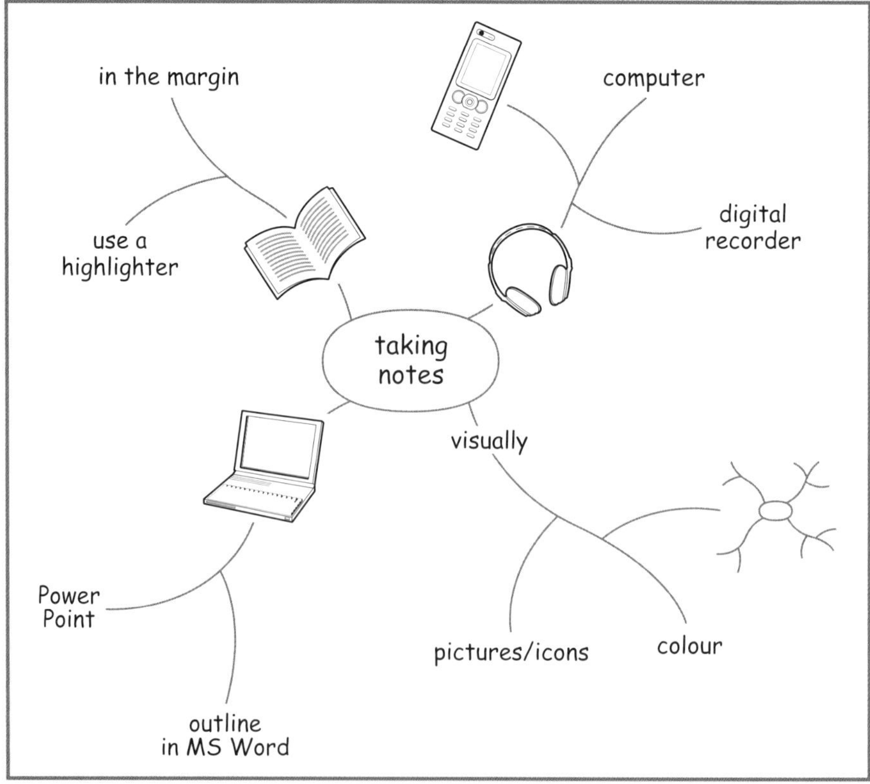

Figure 5 There are many ways to take notes during your studies. OU students are encouraged to write in the margins of their course materials and use highlighters. You can also word process your notes, record your voice using a mobile phone or digital recorder or use mind maps and other visual methods

Take time to explore different approaches to note taking (see Figure 5). You may prefer one approach over others or you may prefer to have a range of styles that you can apply to different activities.

> ‘I use different colours to highlight different types of information. Sometimes I use red for negatives and green for positives, which is useful for assignments. Other times I use different colours for course themes or topics. It all depends.’

Here are some ideas to get you started.

- Use different coloured paper for different topics.
- Try different sizes of paper. A3 is a popular choice as it allows more space in which to create an overview.
- Explore structures such as flow charts, block designs, family trees, spider plans or other forms of mind map.
- Use different coloured pens to help identify and differentiate between topics and subtopics.

Have a look at the list in Table 3 and think about how you might tackle taking notes in each situation.

Table 3 Your approaches to note taking

Activity	Your strategy
reading and summarising	
exams and revision	
during tutorials	
planning assignment answers	
residential school	
listening on phone	
listening to CD or DVD	

How technology can help

Try to explore the tools you already have before looking at others that might require more training and practice.

Computer programs such as Word or Excel offer lots of useful tools. But in addition to computers there are electronic devices such as:

- portable audio devices: digital recorders, mini-disk and tape-recorders
- palmtops and PDAs
- mobile phones.

Organising your notes

Once you have made notes (whether in writing, on your computer or as an audio file) you'll need to keep them organised so that you can find them easily when you need them. The Skills for Study booklet 'Reading and Taking Notes' includes useful advice on getting organised.

Top tips

Good notes should be brief and to the point.

Taking notes helps with active reading. Good notes can help in preparing for assignments or revising for an exam.

Try out different styles of note taking, such as linear notes, spider diagrams or audio notes to help you decide which method is best for you.

Try annotating your course materials with highlighter pens or colour-coded sticky notes.

Assignment writing

Assignment writing can be both challenging and exciting. It involves several different processes such as research, planning, reflection and organisation. It can be a very enjoyable activity that provides an opportunity to develop your thinking and demonstrate your learning.

7.1 The challenges you might face

Students with dyslexia often have very good knowledge and understanding of the course material but can have difficulty organising and structuring this into a piece of written work. You may be able to express yourself well verbally but a lack of confidence in spelling or grammar may interfere with the flow of ideas when writing. Slow writing speed can be frustrating as ideas flow far too quickly to be captured on paper.

> ‘I am learning to stop worrying so much about spelling and that is helping me to think more clearly about what I'm writing. Realising that spelling isn't always the most important thing is very useful. I've also found that using mind maps has really helped me with organising my work.’

7.2 What you can do

Try to gain an overview of the course requirements for assignments. You can do this by:

- investigating how much writing is required in your course
- checking the required type of assignment (for example, report style or essay style assignments)
- reviewing advice about the appropriate style of writing.

Use this information to give you some ideas for organising your own assignment. For example, you could break essays or reports into their different parts (introduction, paragraph one about *x*, paragraph two about *y* etc.) to give you some ideas for planning.

> ‘If a question asks, for example, for three factors affecting something then to make sure I don't forget to include all three I write ‘factor 1’, ‘factor 2’ and ‘factor 3’ at the top of the page. When I have included each factor I cross it off.’

Remember to use any sources of help available to you during writing – your tutor or study adviser, websites, word processing facilities, other students, friends and family, computer conferences, books and study guides, digital recorders.

Plan your time

Be sure to allocate sufficient time for each stage of the writing process – students with dyslexia may need to allow more than the recommended time. Knowing that you have organised your time can minimise some of the stress involved in working to a deadline (see Figure 6).

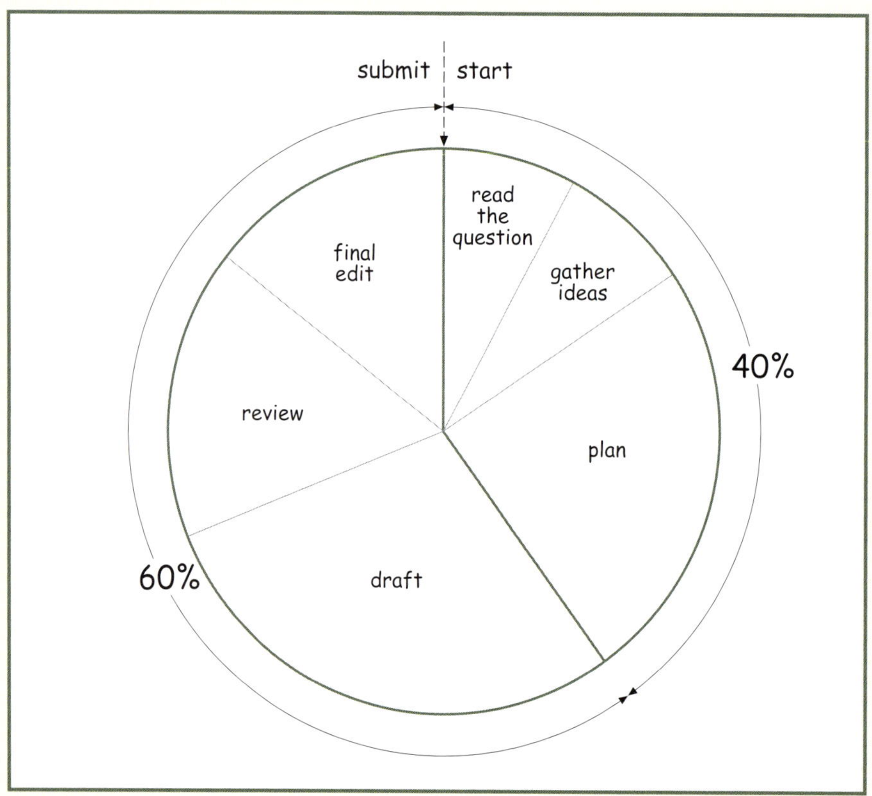

Figure 6 Be sure to allocate enough time to planning how you will approach an assignment before you move on to writing it

Thinking about the stages

Each stage of writing an assignment has a different focus. Knowing what these are can really clarify your thinking (see Table 4).

Table 4 Stages in writing an assignment

Stage	What to do
Reading the question	Identify precisely what you are being asked to do
Gathering ideas	Gather all relevant information (index cards, notes etc.) Decide which illustrations and examples to use
Planning	Produce an overview of all content required (e.g. as a spider plan, mind map, list, notes on PowerPoint) Decide on the overall structure Decide on the basic paragraph structure Group ideas and topics together (e.g. using coloured highlighters)
Drafting	Take each topic separately. Write a list of relevant points, using short and simple sentences
Reviewing	Re-read the question and your draft, and if possible ask someone else to read it for you Check for content and structure
Final edit	Make a final draft, incorporating comments

There are more ideas about preparing assignments on the *Skills for OU Study* website at www.open.ac.uk/skillsforstudy

7.3 Preparing for your next assignment

Using feedback

When your work has been marked, read the feedback carefully. Your tutor's feedback will contain advice and pointers for improving your future work and will help you to learn. Tutors are skilled at giving constructive advice. Make a note of things you would like to improve in your next assignment. If you are unclear about what the comments mean ask your tutor to explain further. Using feedback is an integral part of developing your approach to assignment writing (see Figure 7).

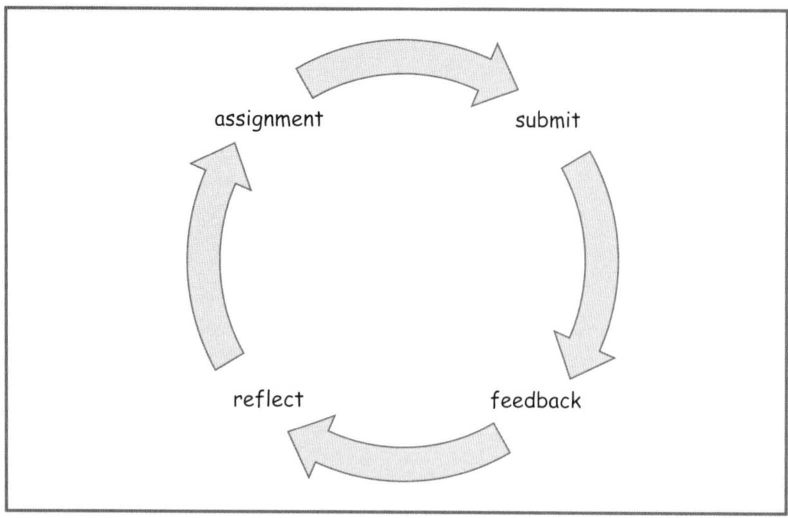

Figure 7 Use the feedback on your assignments to help you improve your writing and study skills in preparation for the next one

Discussion with other students can also give you ideas about good construction and other aspects of composition. General advice and feedback on common mistakes are often given on computer conferences and websites. Seek help on areas of weakness when working on your next assignment.

> ‘When I first started studying I used to just read the mark, but over time I've realised how important the comments on the assignment are. They usually suggest things that I can do that will improve my work for next time, and this is making my marks higher than they were. I also know that I can talk to my tutor if I don't understand any of the comments.’

Spelling

Spelling can be one of the biggest worries, partly because of memories of school: the embarrassment of having to spell out loud or write on the blackboard. Your difficulty with spelling may be that you don't automatically make generalisations, so you have to learn each word individually. You may forget a spelling from one sentence to the next, so that you always have to look it up.

It's not always essential to spell with complete accuracy, unless a wrong spelling changes your meaning (‘nitrate’ for ‘nitrite’, for example). Ask your tutor what level of accuracy is acceptable, and discuss the most helpful way of having your mistakes pointed out.

Information on strategies for learning spellings can be found on the *Skills for OU Study* website at www.open.ac.uk/skillsforstudy

8 Revision and exams

Exams give an indication of your level of expertise in a particular subject. They are not a test of you as a human being, but an opportunity to show what you have learned. If you think you may need exam concessions, such as extra time or approval to use assistive technology, you must complete the form FRF3. Please read the booklet *Meeting Your Exam Needs* (available from your regional or national centre) for more details, or go to the section about examinations on the Services for Disabled Students website at www.open.ac.uk/disability, where you will also find the online FRF3 form and instructions on how to complete it. If you want to apply for exam concessions, complete an FRF3 form and submit it to the OU as early in your course as possible. Exam arrangements are made individually with each student, so allow time for them to be set up. Make a list of things you need to do (see Figure 8) and start to action it as soon as possible.

Good organisation and time management are essential when revising for exams.

Exam date: ....

To do	Date	Done
• submit form, FRF3		
• discuss access arrangement, if necessary	asap	
• go to revision section on web - http://www.open.ac.uk/skillsforstudy	asap	
• order past exam papers	....	
• list topics to revise	....	
• make a timetable	....	
• collate and label notes	ongoing	

Figure 8 Make a list of things you need to do in order to revise effectively before your exam. Keep an eye on your calendar as your exam date approaches

8.1 The challenges you might face

Revision and exams can be difficult and stressful for anyone, especially if the last exam taken was a long time ago. Dyslexia can compound the problems, as all the stresses seem to come together and there is additional pressure on memory skills.

For most courses spelling doesn't matter as long as words are recognisable, but if your spelling deteriorates badly under pressure, you may be able to make arrangements to use a spellchecker.

Look at your specimen exam paper very carefully to find out as much as you can about your own exam and consider if any problems might be caused by its format. Exam questions are of various different types.

- Essays – similar to essays for assignments, but you won't be expected to include so much detail.
- Structured questions with many parts – take care to answer all the parts specified.
- Questions that require short answers, notes or diagrams – practise each type of answer needed, and check with your tutor if you are unsure.
- Multiple-choice questions – these require careful reading as it's easy to be misled by the form of the question even if you have a good understanding of the subject.
- If you have difficulties with the speed of your working memory, you may find it difficult to remember the question while reviewing all the possible answers. Try highlighting the key words in the question before looking at the answer options, or make some notes to help you keep the question clear.

8.2 What you can do

Revision should be a continuous process, which ideally begins as you work your way through the course and which can help you understand the material. There is then a more intense revision period closer to the exam date, probably following your last assignment.

Understanding your memory

Most students find that learning is best done in manageable chunks. Try study periods of 20 to 40 minutes, with breaks of three to ten minutes, but experiment to find your own best pattern. This can vary, depending on your physical and mental state, the time of day and even the weather.

The greatest memory loss is within 24 hours of learning something, so review your learning within that time. If you study during the evening, go over the materials on your way to work the next day. A quick review then will be more useful than a longer one later. Build reviews into your study plan. When revision begins in earnest, say six to eight weeks before the exam, you'll be able to remember more.

Things can be committed to memory more easily if they are:

- brief
- clear
- understood
- multisensory
- repeated
- linked or sequential (recall one thing and others will follow).

Active revision helps you to remember what you have been revising.

Ongoing revision for the course

From the beginning of your studies regularly select essential information from earlier sections of the course. At this stage you are concerned with gathering and organising material more than with learning it. Week by week, use this ongoing revision to assemble the key points of the course. Strategies like using colours to highlight something important, or summarising a key point on a separate page, will help you build up useful materials for later on.

Once you have identified what it is you need to learn you can start to put the materials into a form from which you can learn best. You might like to try mind maps or index cards: you'll find other options in the Revising, examinations and assessment area of the *Skills for OU Study* website at www.open.ac.uk/skillsforstudy

Revision planning for an exam

Make a list of the topics you need to revise, in order of priority. You may have to consider not revising all of them. If you're short of time, remember that you'll cope best with the ones you enjoy most, and may need to leave aside the ones you find most difficult. However, make sure you include the topics that are central to the course. Past papers can be useful to identify which topics come up regularly.

Try fitting your topics onto a timetable or chart. You could see one subject right through in consecutive sessions, or you might prefer to start or finish each revision day with your favourite topic. You can change things as you go, but the benefit of the chart is that you can work through the course systematically, ticking off each topic as you go. You can download a template of this chart from the *Skills for OU Study* website at www.open.ac.uk/skillsforstudy

Before a revision session:

- decide what you are going to revise, using your chart
- plan exactly when, how and what you are going to revise in that session.

During the session:

- break your session into chunks and include time to do different things, which will help you to sustain your interest.

Using past papers

Use past exam papers for practice. It's never too soon to start doing this. Here are some ideas for how to use them.

- Apply the Process, Content, Examples approach (PCE approach) to a question – see below.
- Plan some outline answers. Organise your thoughts by quickly jotting down ideas as they come into your head – brainstorming. Then put them into groups of related ideas. Now put the groups into a logical order. Allow five to ten minutes for this.
- Practise answering some whole questions. After brainstorming and ordering your ideas, practise writing your answer within the time limit for the question.

Decoding questions using the PCE approach

If you can identify what the examiner is asking you to do, you are well on the way to answering the question. The PCE approach gives you a strategy for working this out.

P is for process word

Somewhere in the question you'll find a process word, or a phrase that suggests a process, such as explain, contrast, what is the difference between, evaluate. Highlight the word or phrase in colour or by circling it on the paper.

C is for content

Use a different colour or underlining to highlight the content. Examples of content could be: local government in the 1960s, mitosis, the eradication of smallpox, Eliza Doolittle. There will be a focus. For example, it may want you to discuss the relationship between Eliza and Professor Higgins.

You now have a good idea of what the examiner is asking you, and you have a colour-coded reminder to refer to (see Figure 9).

E is for examples

Your answer will be enriched by relevant examples that support your comments and they will gain you extra marks. They will also add weight to your arguments. Sometimes marks might be set aside specifically for examples.

(*a*) Describe and compare the main ways in which your new work as an HRM specialist might differ from your past experience.

(*b*) (i) Identify and describe the different types of policies and procedures that you regard as a priority to be established within the first year after you start the new job.

(ii) Explain the reasons for your priorities and indicate some of the main objectives for the policies and procedures concerned.

Key:
Process words: what you need to do in your answer
Content words: what your answer should be about

Figure 9 Try using highlighters to colour code the question

Planning how to use your time in the exam

Even if you're allowed extra time you'll still be working to time limits. It's best to work out well beforehand how much time to spend on each question or each part of the paper. Look at your own specimen paper carefully to see how many questions you have to answer, and whether any of them carry a greater percentage of the marks.

Take a simple case as an example. You have a three-hour exam plus 30 minutes extra time. You must answer four questions out of eight, each carrying 25 per cent of the marks. How long should you spend on each question? Try working it out for yourself, then see if you agree with us.

- Allow 10 minutes to read the paper through and decide which questions to answer.
- Allow around 20 minutes at the end to check through the answers.
- 3 hours 30 mins – 30 mins leaves 3 hours.

Divide 3 hours 10 minutes between four questions = 47 minutes for each question, with 2 minutes over. We decided to spend 45 minutes on each question. The exam starts at 2.00 and finishes at 5.30, so:

- start planning and writing Q1 at about 2.10 and stop the first question at 2.55
- start planning and writing Q2 at 2.55 and stop the second question at 3.40
- start planning and writing Q3 at 3.40 and stop the third question at 4.25
- start planning and writing Q4 at 4.25 and stop the fourth question at 5.10
- spend the last 20 minutes checking your answers and making any additions.

Remember, if you are dyslexic you will need to allow extra time to think and plan your answer. This is because you may find it difficult to think and write simultaneously and it is therefore important to clarify your thoughts before focusing on the writing. So, within each question, allow 40% of the time for planning and 60% of the time for writing.

Top tips

Put your watch or a small clock on your table, and stick to the times you've worked out.

Start each answer on a fresh page in the answer book, leaving some space after each answer in case you want to add something later.

8.3 How the OU can help

It is possible that some access arrangements could help you in your exam. As a first step, discuss this with the Disability and Additional Requirements Team at your regional or national centre.

Having the right conditions and facilities for your exam will help to relieve the additional stress that dyslexia can cause. It isn't cheating to have them. Extra time is essential if your reading or writing is slow, and it will give you time to use your planning strategies too. You may also need short rest breaks.

Some of the access arrangement options available for exams include:

- the exam paper in an alternative format, such as printed on coloured paper, in large print, with coloured overlays or provided as an audio recording
- an alternative way to present your answer other than handwriting, such as by word processing, or dictation to a scribe (also known as an amanuensis)
- extra working time or rest breaks.

It's still very important to practise exam techniques beforehand, using past papers if you can. It's also important to practise with your scribe, if you're going to have one.

If over-anxiety is a problem for you there is more information online on Skills for OU Study, where you will also find some downloadable audio material that will help you deal with stress.

There are more ideas about revision and examinations on the *Skills for OU Study* website at www.open.ac.uk/skillsforstudy

In conclusion

For further advice on studying with dyslexia please contact the appropriate person or service from the list below.

OU staff

Staff in the Disability and Additional Requirements Team of your regional or national centre will be happy to discuss your specific needs and how to access any additional support, such as:

- course choice advice
- financial assistance
- individual access arrangements for exams.

Your tutor

All tutors have some information on dyslexia and other specific learning difficulties and will be happy to discuss your approaches to study. However, if specific advice is needed your tutor will refer you to your regional or national centre.

Your StudentHome page

StudentHome (www.open.ac.uk/students) is your starting point for online resources with advice on:

- financial matters
- study skills
- services for students with disabilities – includes information about alternative formats for course materials.

Reference

British Psychological Society, Division of Educational and Child Psychology (BPS) (1999) *Dyslexia, Literacy and Psychological Assessment. Working Party Report,* BPS, Leicester.